Girl, Go Eat A Cookie

...and then handle business!

Tammie T. Polk

*Thank you
for reading!
~ Tammie
Pr. 3:15-18*

Cover designed by Author
Photo Taken by J.D. Westbrook

Tammie T. Polk
Visit my website at www.professionallysassy.me

Printed in the United States of America

First Printing: February 2021
Amazon/KDP

ISBN-13 978-0-578-86512-6

This book is for every woman who has looked at life and wondered if she even wanted to deal with it... May what I've written here give you the strength to take it on! Thank you, Pastor James Butts, for preaching the message that inspired me to get up!

Contents

People often ask me how I make it with everything I do. I tell them that it takes three things: Grace, naps, and COOKIES!

—TAMMIE T. POLK

Introduction

As women, we have a lot of business to handle, making us REAL and TRUE business women whether we realize it or not!

We have to take on life itself, our faith, our families and the demands that come with them, our ministries, our education, and our businesses or careers. It's all EXHAUSTING, isn't it?

Know what else it is? Necessary! Yes, I heard that sigh just now!

My intent with this book is to share something unforgettable that I heard in a sermon recently. The pastor was talking about how Paul, after being stoned and left for dead, picked himself up, went back into the city, and continued to preach Jesus! The title of that message was, "It's Not About Getting Knocked Down, But About Getting Back UP!"

That message stuck with me so much that I broke down in tears, texting my husband while he was there at church live. They weren't tears of sadness, though. I cried because I realized just how much God had done for me.

2020 dealt me the toughest hand of cards I'd ever seen! From February to September, my family grew to know God and His grace even more as we saw person after person leave us stranded.

February to August was my battle with what we thought was multiple sclerosis, which was scary for me and I had no one but God to depend on in those doctor's offices. I went through three MRIs, two CT scans, over twenty blood test, nosebleeds, two musculoskeletal heart attacks, three rounds of prednisone and hydrocodone combined, a spinal tap, loss of the use of my hands, difficulty walking, and extreme fatigue.

Then, in late August, my husband was involved in a car accident that totaled the one form of transportation we had. By the grace of GOD, he walked away, but it was tough for him as he had to file for FMLA leave because he couldn't get any help.

Even in this, we experienced God's matchless GRACE!

Despite the constant pain and agony that I was in, God allowed me to meet my goal of publishing 125 book by my birthday, which is August 11th. I didn't let what was going on with my hands keep me from reaching that goal.

I was blessed because I had friends who stepped up and said they would type for me because they didn't want to see me quit. God gave me peace despite being attacked in my dreams by the thoughts of not finishing...

I'll stop there because I will have written the entire book in this one chapter LOL!

This book is about looking at life and all that it's throwing at you and saying, "I've got business to handle."

Grace, Naps, and Cookies!

You may chuckle at these three things, but they matter more to our lives, faith, families, ministries, education, and business than we think.

This can be a book all by itself and, if you are familiar with me at all, you already know it's in the works, but I had to include a tidbit of it here!

Allow me to take you on a journey and show you why these things are SO important.

First, grace—this is more than the prayer that we say over our food. It is the one thing, as you will see in the following chapter, that we receive from God and give to others, yet we leave ourselves out.

How? By thinking that we have to be perfect in all of these areas, and it's killing us both inside and out... Even though we already know that, we soldier on as to say that the increase effort we give it is going to make it better. Would you believe me if I told you that not giving yourself grace actually makes things WORSE?! I need to move on before I give too much away here.

Second, naps—we hated them growing up and have been apologizing for our attitudes ever since! Sometimes we, just like our children, need to sit down somewhere and chill the heck out before somebody goes missing! Gone are the days of Team No Sleep.

Sweetheart, I KNOW how TIRED you are, but do you use those few quiet moments to simply close your eyes? Have you poured enough into your family that you can say you need to lay down and you won't wake up to Armageddon?

The stress that you feel...

The angst that worries you...

The headache that keeps coming back...

All of these are signs that you need a NAP! Throw out the statistics that say naps break your sleep cycle and do what works for YOU! I know a doctor who said this in a workshop and she has since RECANTED, starting to take naps herself! Whether it's ten minutes or an hour, please take a moment to close your eyes and let whatever it is roll off from you.

Finally, COOKIES—you may not be a cookie connoisseur as I am, but they help. Yes, I know you're trying to get right with JESUS and cookies are a stumbling block to you, but you might need a good one from time to time.

I am known to have at least nine different types of store bought and bakery prepared cookies in my house at one time! My favorite local bakery knows exactly what to do for me when I walk in, too! Although it's a hilarious thought, cookies have a purpose.

A cookie is anything that gives you the strength to power through when times are tough. For some, it's music or a message. For others, it might be that good ole, southern fried, filled with all of GOD'S calories and fat grams, nap inducing comfort food that makes you the stingiest person on Earth. Whatever your pick me up may be, that's your cookie.

Okay...We've laughed and eye rolled enough. We've got to get into the main message of this book.

See you in the next chapter!

Grace...and three types of it!

God gives it to us, we give it to others, but we don't give it to ourselves.

And he said unto me, My grace is sufficient for thee: for my
strength is made perfect in weakness...
—2 Corinthians 12:9a

*W*onderful grace of our loving Lord... Grace that exceeds our sin and our guilt...

If you know that particular hymn, I'm sure you know what comes next. Here's the thing that we miss—God give us grace, we give it to others, but we don't give it to ourselves.

As I said in the introduction to the book, we really don't understand how grace works sometimes. We think that, because we have a problem or two, grace is the furthest thing from us. Allow me to remind you that it's not!

If you are able to do anything about what's going on in your life, faith, family, ministry, education, business, or career, that's grace! Where do you think that amazing idea you thought of or someone gave you came from? God gave you the grace to calm down enough to either be able to think of the idea or be able to receive and use the idea presented to you. How many times have we had a revelation and said, "Look at God" or "Won't He do it"? Grace made that happen!

Being able to pray about it to a Holy God is grace...

Being able to turn to the inspired Word of God for comfort and encouragement in the midst of a trial is grace...

Having someone to call, if only to cry is grace...

We completely misunderstand how much grace God gives us daily! I'm not talking about the grace of forgiveness for sin or keeping us from danger. I'm talking about the grace to not go crazy in crisis!

How many times has God brought something from your past back to your remembrance that helped you to make it through the day, make money, make something out of almost nothing—if you're not shouting from that grace right now, stop reading!

I will never forget the day that I found twenty-two dollars in an old tote bag that was in a closet at my childhood home. My mother had passed away and my family and I found ourselves in a dark time where we had to move back into the house. God gave grace there because my stepfather did NOT have to do that for us!

I needed to get minutes for my cell phone to be able to communicate and I didn't have the money. Something told me to start looking through my old stuff. There in the mesh pockets of a tote bag I'd carried as a teenager was twenty-two dollars wrapped up in a Walgreens receipt.

This was 2009 and the date on the bills was 1996. I was extremely nervous when I went to the store because I didn't think that the counterfeit pen would even work on the bills because they were so old! In my heart, I begged God to let this work because we had no other means of communication at the time. It worked and I ran out of the store before anything else happened.

To me, that was God showing grace in a tough time. We'd just lost everything we had and needed to rebuild—this was needed help that wasn't going to come from anywhere nor anyone else.

That's what the grace God gives us to survive and thrive does! We can't see who, what, when, where, why, how, nor how much, but He can and then turns around and gives us the grace to take it all in and handle it.

He gives us grace when we need Him...

He gives us grace when we need others...

He gives us grace when we're stupid...

He simply gives us grace!

Were it not for grace....

The second area of grace I want to talk about is the grace that we give others. Now, I will say here that there are times when we give people WAY too much grace! We give so much grace that we make excuses for the level of grace we've given. We have to make that level of grace make sense when we know that we should be giving tough love instead. Then, we get mad when that grace is purposely misused and trampled on!

People have a homing device for extreme grace givers, especially if they have the gift of gab. There are those we encounter who know how to tug at our heartstrings just so that fountain of grace opens to overflowing. No matter how much giving them that grace hurts or puts us in a bind, we continue to pour it out like water, not holding them accountable for anything that they've said or done.

This type of grace is dangerous and has even gotten people killed! It's time to open your eyes and see that person is poking holes in your good nature and will drain you! You can't give everyone the same level of grace, either. There are some who, no matter how much grace you grant, will show you that doing so was the worst decision you could have EVER made!

Think about the woman or man caught up in an abusive relationship. They've given so much grace that they can't even tell that they're doing it anymore. They fall for every gift and every apology because it's something that they like or makes them feel good.

Not all of them reach their breaking point and say enough is enough...some of them find themselves in the arms of Jesus because of the amount of grace that they gave.

Think about the woman or man dealing with an unfaithful spouse. They have Biblical cause to leave, yet they continue to give grace simply because they either came back or never left despite what they were doing.

Like the abused, not all of them reach their breaking point...some of them come home and find the side piece sitting on the coach, pregnant, or otherwise.

Yes, the Bible tells us to live peaceably with all men, but it also says for us to separate from and mark unruly people, too!

My love, grace is a precious commodity...protect it!

The final area I want to get into is not giving ourselves grace. Listen, even Adam and Eve failed at perfection and were still given a measure of grace.

I understand that you want everything to run smoothly, but you must realize that every speed bump isn't meant to stop you! You may need to slow down and revise, revamp, refocus, and change some things.

I know that you want to be seen as the baddest when it comes to your home and family, but trust me when I say that the woman you are comparing yourself to is having the same struggles you are! She simply wears them differently. If you catch her on the right day, you'll see that she's no different from you and just might have it worse than you, but she makes certain you NEVER know!

What you are stressing over to gain, she may be stressing over possibly losing, so watch yourself here.

Do you want to know why I chose the verse I did for this chapter? It's because so many of us are JUST like Paul! We have something that is weighing us down and we want to be rid of it, but we can't be for whatever reason.

Like Paul, we cry out to God, call every doctor, phone every friend, use every essential oil, and follow the advice of any guru who even smells like they know what they're talking about because we want RELIEF!

He says, "My grace is SUFFICIENT", meaning that it's enough... The same grace He gives you, you need to give it to yourself. We read stories of struggle all the time and say that it won't be us and we're going to make sure that it's not, but life doesn't always work out that way because we're human and we deal with other humans.

"But, Tammie, I have so much to do!" Yes, we all do, but you're headed right for a Psalms 23 shutdown. You need to give yourself the grace to rest, to not be okay, and to not know all of the answers. Let's park right here awhile.

The grace to rest is often the hardest because of the demands placed on our lives. How so? Keep reading....

We run ourselves into the ground for jobs, clients, and customers who only care about themselves being able to move forward.

We deal with people flipping out because we want to take a day off during a busy time and know that they know we deserve that time.

We are trying to be lighthouses and examples of triumph to the children in our lives who are in turn telling us to let them learn and do because we won't always be there for them.

We are the first to get to church and leave after the last ones to leave because the work of God must go forth.

We pull all-nighters as we are trying to study to help our children the next day, finish that assignment for the degree we finally have time to go back and get, or even to meet a deadline at work.

We don't give ourselves intentional grace in our own lives and then complain when everyone around us is thriving and growing and we're looking like the grumpy cat from YouTube!

GIRL, GO EAT A COOKIE...AND THEN HANDLE BUSINESS!

You are allowed be tired...and the day that you're not is the day things around you need to change!

The grace to not be okay is one that is under attack today and seen as a dirty word or phrase.

One of my favorite social media quotes said, "I'm allowed to be a masterpiece and a work in progress at the same time. Truer words have never been spoken!

STOP BEING THE STRONG ONE FOR EVERYBODY BUT YOU!

If you're anything like me, you spend an inordinately unholy amount of time thinking about who is not there for you when you are having a not okay moment. Because this is true, you decide that you're going to feign as though you are okay so no one will know how much that affected you.

Giving yourself the grace to be okay becomes lying to yourself as to how unbothered you are about what's going on with you. You will take your big girl pill, pull up your big girl panties, pull up your bootstraps and push it to the back of your mind. Then, when someone whom you know truly cares about you comes along your mind says, "Why are YOU asking me if I am okay? You're just like everyone else... you don't care about me," and then you give them a pacifying answer. You feel that you can't open up to them because nothing will change.

When you stop pouting like a five year old and deal with the fact that you're not okay, one of the first things you'll do is go for a cookie—remember what I said a cookie is, though! You NEED to turn to what makes YOU feel better in that moment and don't worry about ANYONE ELSE who is not DIRECTLY affected by you not handling business.

The problem with giving yourself graces is that you feel like you can't, but who is saying that? You are not meant to push through everything and show a brave face!

Take the time to rest and nurse that cold you feel coming up on you!

Go to the doctor and take the S off your chest, tell them what's going on, and get the help you need.

Go on that vacation you've scheduled and don't alter it for anyone else's purpose that is not within your four walls or and is not an aging parent in need of care.

Take that day off work and turn your phone off!

Don't only use your nights for housework and business tasks you couldn't get done earlier in the day.

Grace...and three types of it! Now, I want you to go to grab your cookie, go to the workbook, and empty out until you feel the need to take a deep breath—then keep going!

Grit...and her twin sister, Grind!

A woman's strength is like NONE on Earth, but we have to remember it's there!

But by the grace of God I am what I am: and his grace which was bestowed upon me was not vain; but I laboured more abundantly than they all: yet not I, but the grace of God which was with me.
—*1 Corinthians 15:10*

*P*aul was absolutely INSANE, right? I know many of us have read this story and wondered why in ALL of God's ETERNAL creation he would get up and go back into the city where he was stoned and left for dead, but how many times have we done the same?

You fight battles daily that most people would have given up on because you know that making a difference and impact in that place is necessary for your life, faith, family, ministry, education, and business or career to be what it is MEANT to be! You put on that brave face, clean up the bumps and bruises, and go right back in for Round Two.

Why? It's because you understand the necessity of doing so! You pray and ask God to help you develop the tunnel vision you need and to close your mouth before something He would NOT be pleased with comes out of your mouth.

Think about your job or business for a second. I want you to name that ONE coworker, boss, or client who makes you want to turn in your two weeks' notice eighteen months early or close your business altogether.

You want to tell them off and cut them off SO bad, but self-control got the better of you, right? Let me tell you why that is!

Like Paul, you know that you have a mission and assignment with that person that still has to be accomplished despite how they treat you. He didn't go back into the city to tell them off, but to share God's message with them ONE MORE TIME before God stepped in on them!

You see, the reason you have to go back in there is because you know EXACTLY what that person is about to go through. Even though it may be unavoidable, you want to walk away with a clear conscience, knowing that YOU did YOUR part to ensure that it was as soft of a blow as could be, yet the fact that they didn't listen has NOTHING TO DO WITH YOU!

Now that we've gotten that out of the way, let's make this thing personal...

Life has dealt you a hand that has made faith, family, ministry, education, business and career seem like eighteen megaton weights on your shoulders. Forget cinder blocks—you are laid flat out on the ground wishing you could MOVE!

You start to feel that nothing you do will EVER work, so you take whatever Life decided you can have....

GIRL, GO EAT A COOKIE...AND THEN HANDLE BUSINESS!

You may not be able to do everything you want to do about your situation, but that doesn't mean that you sit back and take whatever comes—you are TOO important and valuable to have that mindset!

The people who are trying to lovingly shake some sense into you are there for a reason, just as Elijah was with the widow of Zarephath. She thought he was a madman when he asked her to make a cake for him first—all she saw was what she thought she'd didn't have. Here was a man of God telling her to trust God and she STRUGGLED.

The key here is that she OBEYED and was BLESSED! When you take one step, God will take three, but you have to take the step in order to see Him move in any way!

You are to trust Him, do what is in your power to do and trust Him to provide the rest—but that's not what we do!

We either go spaghetti mode like a child or we start to grit and grind so hard that God doesn't stand a Holy Spirit of a chance to do what He needs to do in your life so that the other areas fall in line. We limit God either way, not understanding that He needs to see our grit and grind, but in the right way.

We wouldn't have much of the Bible had Paul NOT gotten up... it would have ended right there when he got up and then left the next day.

I know that you're not Paul, but please understand that there is going to be someone somewhere sometime somehow someway who needs to know something about overcoming what you are currently facing. I've seen it too many times!

You may have to do some things that you don't like or know how to do well, but that's what the grace of God and having the right support system with will handle on your behalf. You aren't by yourself—Hebrews tells us that.

What you don't want to do is turn into Saul and move before you are supposed to and mess something up royally. Yes, what happened to him can happen to you and it will wreak havoc in your life, faith, family, ministry, education, business, or career—trust me! Let me break that down.

Your life will become so ingrained and inundated with the grit and grind that you start to show your family that they don't have to trust God. Yes, you may start flourishing due to your efforts, yet something on the inside will say, "God could have and would have given you much more than this had you let Him." You know that still small voice is right, but you go right back to it.

"So, Tammie, what am I supposed to do?" I'm glad you asked. There is a quote going around from a rapper that says this, "I don't want to move fast. I want to move correctly." Believe it or not, that's exactly what we ought to do!

Handling business in your life, faith, family, ministry, education, business or career is about moving CORRECTLY!

Are you talking to the RIGHT people?

Do you know that you are supposed to be getting done?

Do you know when it needs to be done?

Have you found out where you need to go?

Have you checked the motives behind your grit and grind?

Do you know what action steps you need to take to make this happen?

Do you know how much time, money, and work needs to be done so that the outcome you want is produced?

We mess up when ANY of this gets out of whack! Why do you think we always see quotes or overhear conversations about not sharing what you're working with or going through with people who won't understand? It's because we are going full grit and grind too fast and missing out on the quality!

There's no shortcut to baking a cake nor handling business. When you start cutting corners, it will become noticeable right away!

Your ministry will never see the growth, progress, or impact that's needed because you are too busy "doing the work" to see what's NOT working. By the time you do, there's ZERO chance for damage control because people, places, things, and ideas have all gone out the window. Now you're blaming your team instead of looking at the leadership, which is YOU!

Your education will suffer as well because, no matter if it's something personal or professional, you'll overlook the requirements for a project and think that your way of doing it is better. Then, when there are points taken off or you don't a favorable response from the work you've done, you blame them and will even lie and say that those requirements weren't there at first. Now, your business or career is affected because you've lost out on key knowledge that would have taken you a LOT further.

Grit and her twin sister Grind both require BALANCE! I know, feel, and understand that you plunge forward with one on each shoulder, but you have to be careful!

Everyone around you knows your work ethic and your hustle, whether they say so or not. The problem comes in when you let either one of them go into hyperdrive! Paul didn't...he went back into the city, finished his work, and moved on.

You have to ask yourself what business it is you need to handle, focus on that, and then move on! Too many of us carry the load of others and share our grit and grind when we don't need to do so.

Finally, I want to address apathy and laziness. I've said a little about this above, but I want to ensure that you understand that neither has any place in the business you're endeavoring to handle! When you allow yourself to become apathetic and lazy because you feel as though the grit and grind you give won't matter, you are hurting yourself and setting yourself up for failure that doesn't have to occur.

Stop looking at what you don't have...

Stop talking about how hard it is...

Stop lying about what's going on...

Stop bribing your family to keep up appearances...

Stop saying that there's nothing you can do...

If that were true, then the mission wouldn't have been given to you. You sound a lot like Moses right now and, trust me, you don't want God talking to you like God talked to him!

Do you want apathy and laziness to be what your friends, family, loved ones, church members, frenemies, enemies, and foes see? Now you may throw me a side eye on those last three, but TRUST ME, what you are showing them is nothing but ammunition that they can and WILL use against you! There are people waiting for you to stop, give up, and throw in the towel.

As another favorite quote of mine says, "Who are you making right by giving up on your dreams?" Throughout the Bible, we find examples of different people saying this was going to happen. The same happens in our lives when we are lazy and apathetic. When things get out hand, you'll be dealing with "I told you so" while in tears because you didn't see the necessity of getting back up after being stoned nearly to death.

If God has allowed you to get up from it, you are slapping Him in the face if you do so and give up! To be honest, this is one of the reasons why I fought so hard in 2020... I didn't want to disappoint HIM!

As I listened to the pastor present this message, I thought about all of the times that God held me together as I wrote and cried. He kept my mind right despite all of the medication going into my system. He kept me strong when one side of my body completely quit. He strengthened our oldest daughter as she cried and prayed while taking care of her sisters in my stead. He let my husband walk away from an accident and be able to come home to his family hours later.

I know that MY God allowed me to get up and I've have been just like Paul ever since. I know that He raised me up because I still had work to do, so I got after it! You need to do the same because every day that He allows you to wake up is another chance to do what He has put in your head and heart to do—another chance to eat a cookie and then handle business!

I didn't want to do the twenty-seven audio books I did. I wanted to be able to do what I'm doing right now and sit up typing and laughing at what comes out of my brain onto the computer screen. Want to know what kept me from quitting? It was a dream...

In the dream, I felt like I was in the chapter of Hebrews that reminds us about the great cloud of witnesses. I saw everyone who was rooting for me, some I knew and some I didn't. I stood up in the midst of them and said that my condition had gotten the best of me, so I wouldn't be able to finish the course I set out on. As I lifted my head from the copout I'd made, every single person was crying.

It was then that I noticed two faces that sent shockwaves through me—my mother, Terri, and my daughter, Natalynn, both of whom now rest with Jesus. My baby walked up to me and said, "Mommy, you can't quit...I love you. Please don't quit." She touched my hands and then my neck, telling me I had everything I needed.

I woke from that dream at 9:30 PM CST, grabbed my laptop, and went to my couch. I pulled up the list of books I had yet to complete, opened the Audacity recording app, and started talking! I did those audios in FOUR DAYS! I had great accountability partners who wanted to know my progress no matter what time I finished and I gave my report each night.

When I got ready to go to bed after finishing, I felt my waist tighten. I turned because I thought my oldest was hugging me, but no one was there. I smiled because I knew exactly who it was...and I got the best sleep of my life that night.

Grit...and her twin sister Grind! Now, I want you to go to grab your cookie, go to the workbook, and empty out until you feel the need to take a deep breath—then keep going!

Growth...in yourself and others around you!

Your progress isn't just for you!

Howbeit, as the disciples stood round about him, he rose up, and came into the city: and the next day he departed with Barnabas to Derbe.
—Acts 14:20

The ability to get up after a knockdown in your life, faith, family, ministry, education, business, or career isn't about you doing so. There is someone standing around you who needs to know and see that getting up is possible! Your progress isn't always about YOU!

GRIL, GO EAT A COOKIE...AND THEN HANDLE BUSINESS!

The disciples standing around a near lifeless Paul were waiting to see what Paul would do and, no doubt, they thought Jesus had taken his brain cells when he headed back into the same city that stoned him. Yet, he had to...for them.

See, getting up after a knockdown is not always for YOU to be the one to give the testimony—catch that! The testimony of overcoming a situation won't always be told by the person who overcame it because the story of those standing around them might be the REAL testimony!

There is ALWAYS someone watching out of the need to know what to do or how to move. Everyone witnessing you rising above is there to try and find the stray thread that will unravel all that God has strengthened and blessed you to overcome! There is someone who is ready to give up, but they heard that YOU were dealing with it, so they joined the crowd with baited breath hoping to see some sort of solution.

"But Tammie, how does this fight fit all of the areas you're talking about? Does it really apply to all of them?" It most certainly does...and I'll tell you how and why.

One thing my Mom always told me was that, although I am married, my children will look to ME to know what to do next. I didn't understand how true that was until I stopped working full-time due to my husband's work schedule changing.

Our daughters were ten and under at the time and this was a shift because I was home now and my husband was going in earlier. We were a one-income household now, too, and I could tell that my oldest was worried, even as young as she was.

Wanna know what they saw Mommy do? They saw me build my first business, Choice Home Education Consulting. She watched me take $700 and get an online business up and going.

Ladies, your babies and many others are watching how you maneuver through this thing called Life. Why do you think we Google so much stuff? It's because we have a life problem and pray to

Almighty GOD that SOMEBODY has come up with some sort of hack, tip, tool, product, or service that can help us solve our problem. The children in our lives look for what they feel is impossible and we become miracle workers and superheroes to them when we get up from being stoned in life!

That routine you built...

That meal plan you created...

That ancient family life hack you resurrected...

That light bulb that FINALLY came on...

None of it is for YOU alone! Why do you think Paul fusses at mature Christians in the Bible for still needing to be taught when they should be teaching others? It was because they had learned from him in his walk and there were people suffering because they didn't!

Well...I just took care of life, family, faith, and ministry all at the same time, didn't I? Let's move on!

Many of us are also fighting to finish our education. For reasons sometimes beyond our control, we had to let that go for the sake of our family or other area spoken of here. There is a reason that you're fighting so hard—there is someone in your life whom you want to show that it is possible to FINISH!

You're fighting for that growth because it is going to enrich someone's life, faith, family, ministry, education, business, or career simply because you fought to finish. You know that there are opportunities out there that are waiting for you held by people who are pacing holes in the floor hoping that you will finish soon because you are the best person to take hold of that opportunity.

Yes, it's tough...

Yes, math has completely changed from what you knew before...

Yes, you are in classes with children the age of your own children...

I'll say it again: GIRL, GO EAT A COOKIE...AND THEN HANDLE BUSINESS!

You are shining a light into the darkness overtaking the heart and mind of someone else who feels that they will NEVER be able to finish.

Life... faith... family... ministry... education... now business and career, which I talked about a little already.

One of the things I talk about a lot is how opportunities to grow are presented to us and we are too comfortable where we are to see that said opportunities are beneficial to us. We become roses in concrete whose roots have nowhere to go because the concrete laid on us by us is so thick that we give up trying to push any further through it.

Then, it happens...

Someone connected to know seizes said opportunity and you watch as her life, faith, family, ministry, education, business, or career takes off and you're telling yourself that it COULDN'T have been from THAT.

"She had to be doing something else! You're not going to make me believe that sitting in a chair for eight hours straight for two weeks and doing all of those presentations and watching all of those videos led to THAT!"

What you don't understand is that there was someone present who was looking for you and you weren't there, but SHE was. So, the opportunity and energy that was present for you is now in the hands of someone else who is connected to you. You lost out because you made your growth all about YOU!

YOU didn't want to get up THAT early...

YOU didn't want to sit in a chair or in front of a computer for THAT long...

YOU didn't want to pay THAT much money...

YOU focused on what YOU aren't good at and may not do well...

YOU told YOURSELF that you were BETTER OFF without THAT...

Yet, you can't stand to see her coming because she is showing you how much growth you COULD have had if you had only stopped thinking about YOURSELF!

Let me take it back to the personal for a second...

Think about the woman who is working two jobs and going to school in between or after. You think she's crazy until you ask her why she's doing it.

"I want something better for me and my kids. I don't want them to only see the mistakes I made." THAT is when you know that your growth is no longer about YOU—desiring to be an inspiration and an example becomes more important than anything.

Now, I'm not telling you to be fake, phony, or super pseudo spiritual. I understand that getting up takes time and you have some things that you have to heal from and work through first before you can even think about fixing your brain cells to focus on someone else. I get it, but what we often do is use that as an excuse to not do what we can and is in our power to do at that moment.

Paul was doing what God told him to do.

He was stoned for it.

They threw him out of the city, leaving him for dead.

The disciples stood around until he gave a signal that he was still alive.

They helped him up and dusted him off, asking him if he was okay and what he wanted to do next.

In pain, he turned and walked back toward the city!

You may marvel at that, but have you ever wondered what would've happened had he gone the other way? I've mentioned that before, but I want you to keep that at the forefront of your mind.

Why?

PAUL WAS EXPECTED TO GIVE UP AFTER WHAT HE WENT THROUGH, NOT GROW FROM IT AND KEEP GOING!

People have the same expectation of YOU! I don't care how close they are to you nor how saved they may be. On the inside, they are battling with having this expectation because of the gravity of your situation.

They won't come out and TELL you to give up, but you'll notice that they always seem to have a Plan B for you. All of the ideas that they give you is just smoke and mirrors! Neither of them is going to lead to you growing through your situation. They are meant to simulate growth, but they are empty time fillers that will take your further away from your goal.

If you choose to listen to them, you will cause tumultuous times for everyone involved and they will eventually throw you overboard as the men on the ship did Jonah. They don't see the ramifications of taking you away from your growth.

They don't have to live with the results of that happening, but you do. All they will see is the results and will excuse away their role in what you're going through.

Part of growth is auditing your circle, which is also not just about you. It serves to show others the need to do the same while letting them know who they need to let go of and why! You will NOT get to the level of growth that you want to achieve if you have the same people around you now and in the future or that you had around you when you were born.

GROWTH BREEDS SEPARATION AND NOT STAGNATION!

It is said that you are the sum of the five people you hang around with most. The person who came up with that spent a lot of time auditing and rebuilding their circle because they had to so they could move forward in life!

It's the same for you! It's not about keeping loyalties, either, because those close to you can also bring you down further. It will hurt to let them go, but for the sake of the life, faith, family, ministry, education, business, or career you are MEANT to have, they have to be moved to the nosebleeds and watch!

Growth...and what it's REALLY about! Now, I want you to go to grab your cookie, go to the workbook, and empty out until you feel the need to take a deep breath—then keep going!

Gratitude...and how we often miss it!

No matter the circumstance, gratitude goes a long way!

And I thank Christ Jesus our Lord, what hath enabled me, for that he counted me faithful, putting me into the ministry.
—1 Timothy 1:12

hank you and please are often the first things that we are taught to say. How many times have you gotten in trouble for not saying it or had something taken away from you because you didn't say it? I know that I have and I have done this to my children.

Why?

It is because gratitude goes a long way! No matter what we may go through in life, faith, family, ministry, education, business, or career, God is ALWAYS shielding us from SOME type of unseen and unfelt danger or negative consequence. There is something that you wouldn't have been able to do had that person, place, thing, or idea still been present in your life, but you don't see that at first.

If you're anything like me, you find yourself angry over the fact that whatever it is no longer exists. You can't understand why because it was a good thing and it was helping you, so why would someone, especially God, take that away from you?

He did it because it was in the way of you being grateful! There are times when good things can cause problems. Good things can cause us to forget the people, places, things, and ideas that have gotten us to where we are. We will start to look at US and what WE did that was SO good!

Oh, and don't let us get reminded that it had nothing to do with US, but with the GRACE OF GOD! We can't say anything out of fear of God striking us down right where we stand. We stay quiet because we are allowing ourselves to find a way to take the glory for our growth away from him, forgetting who we were and where our ability to overcome originated.

That is why Paul said he was grateful for God allowing him to go into the ministry. This man made his money and achieved his status with the blood of God's people! He took pride in the rulers' satisfaction with him imprisoning and crucifying Christians. He thought he was doing the world a favor by ridding them of these incessant Christians, laughing and mocking them as he carted them away to prison or the cross.

The fact that God didn't take him like He took Enoch is a marvel to most, even me! God had to show him that he wasn't who he thought he was and He, along with others He may send to confirm, will do the same for you! You don't get to claim what God has done. He has a lot of fun with ungrateful people. I mean that loosely, but you get the point.

Think about a spouse or friend who has died. They were perfectly healthy and the fact that they died suddenly baffles you. Then God calls to your remembrance how you talked to them, how you treated them, how you took advantage of them, how you took them for granted, how you used them...despite all that THEY did for YOU! They died because you weren't grateful for them.

Think about why your spiritual walk seems like you are running a constant marathon. You don't know what changed. Then God shows you how your Bible has more dust on it than half the stuff in your attic, how many times you've missed church for no reason, how it's been five years since you told someone about Him, how you are the first person to leave when church is over and the last person to sign up to help when something is needed, and how you now think prayer is worthless...despite all that HE has done for YOU! You feel like He moved because you have LOST your gratefulness for Him.

What about that spouse or child who, all of a sudden, has an attitude with you and no longer talks to you. You wonder what's wrong with THEM and that's how you approach the situation — as if THEY are the problem. Then they remind you of the events in THEIR life you weren't there for, how you waved them away or overreacted when they needed to talk to you, how you criticized everything they said or did even when they were right...despite the fact that they have ALWAYS been there for you! Their attitude is in direct response to the fact that you are no longer grateful for them.

Your ministry also suffers when there is unchecked ungratefulness! If you see that those whom God has blessed you to serve start falling away, know that part of that has to do with the fact that you haven't done more than TELL them that you're grateful for them! When was the last time you made a time, money, or effort sacrifice for THEIR benefit and not JUST yours? Can they recall a time when they FELT like you appreciated them? Their falling away is a sign that you aren't grateful for them.

This applies to your education as well in that those in administration have given you a second chance to finish what you've started. You get in there and get going, but soon wonder why your professors aren't as understanding as they were at the beginning. Then you see that you haven't been putting your best foot forward. You've done just enough to get by and then asked for grace because you know what you turned in was a hot unholy eternal mess that made absolutely no sense to you, let alone anyone else. You started being late with assignments and then get mad because you got the grade that you deserved. It's all THEIR fault, not the fact that you aren't grateful enough for the opportunity. When you are TRULY grateful, nothing that you're asked to do is an issue because you realize that this chance didn't have to be granted to you.

Customer and employee appreciation are often the things left lacking when it comes to our businesses and careers. How many of you have worked with a boss who always looked at what you did as what you are EXPECTED to do? Or you've been told that your paycheck is your appreciation. It makes you feel as though they don't value you, right? Now, put yourself in the boss' place—do you do this to the people who work with, for, or alongside you? They want to know that they matter to you as much as your bottom line does.

Your customers need it, too, business woman! Loyalty and point programs, coupons, or even special occasion greetings go a LONG way with people. Having this allowed me to achieve a major goal...I've got to tell this story.

A packaging company was trying to regain my business after I mentioned that the deals they offered weren't really deals because shipping and tax made it the same price. I didn't feel that happy feeling of having a discount and they didn't like that.

When it came time for my annual birthday discount, instead of giving me fifteen percent off of my order, they gave me fifty DOLLARS off my order with no minimum spending requirement. At the time, I was fantasizing about having my Every Woman Is A Business Woman 30 Day Planner Kit Boxes. I'd held on to the box design for two years because ONE box was sixty dollars...and now I was able to get it!

That spoke volumes to me because this conglomerate of a company revamped their rewards program based off of what I and a few others said to them—that's gratitude and appreciation!

I see you over there questioning why you kept reading and I know you want to put the book down, but I want to challenge you even further.

GIRL, GO EAT A COOKIE...AND THEN HANDLE BUSINESS!

No one wants to deal with someone who is ungrateful in ANY way! You know that you don't want to, yet you don't see why others around you are acting the same way. Believe me when I say that God will take ANYTHING away from you that you aren't grateful for, no matter what it is. You're asking Him why and He's showing you, but how you treated what He blessed you with is more important than you think.

Paul didn't take his call and charge from God lightly and he dealt with a lot of backlash because people didn't believe that God could ever nor would ever use someone like him.

Paul went so far as to say that he was grateful to experience the ridicule that he'd doled out over the years. Remember that Paul was accomplished, highly educated, and a skilled craftsman who was good with his hands. He stood in a place of prominence, yet God had to humble him and He will humble you as well...and it's going to hurt.

Strained relationships...

Job loss...

Missed opportunities...

These are just a few things that you can lose out on by being ungrateful...

Gratitude...and how we often miss it! Now, I want you to go to grab your cookie, go to the workbook, and empty out until you feel the need to take a deep breath—then keep going!

Graduation Day...Finally!

It will all come together...you'll see!

For I am now ready to be offered, and the time of my departure is at hand. I have fought a good fight, I have finished my course, I have kept the faith: Henceforth there is laid up for me a crown of righteousness, which the Lord, the righteous judge, shall give me at that day: and not to me only, but unto all them also that love his appearing.
—2 Timothy 4:6-8

This passage is normally read at memorials and funerals, yet it can give us hope in our life, faith, family, ministry, education, business or career while we are still alive! It's not going to be easy to reach Graduation Day, but OH when you do, there will be nine million reasons to shout.

Although Paul was about to die, he still gave Timothy hope, just as he gives us. There will be a day when God allows us to move to the next level in each of these areas. You won't always be in debt or have a shaky relationship with Him or have a house full of loud children or struggle with difficult Christians or have to take a break from that degree AGAIN or deal with ruthless bosses and annoying coworkers or deal with stressful clients — the time for your departure is at hand because something better has been offered to you.

The problem is that we as women fear Graduation Day because we have poured so much into so many that we can't fathom the thought of no longer having to do that. I remember watching a movie about the Temptations and they went back to visit the mother of one of the singers.

She knew they were coming, so she cooked for them and ended up cooking on automatic and making everything that everyone liked. She admitted that it was hard for her to just cook for HER because she was so used to having a house full of hungry young men trying to make it in the music industry. Her house was a home away from home for them. She didn't know how to switch once those days were no more. Many of us battle with this everyday.

We have poured our souls, blood, sweat, and tears into those God has placed in our path to love on and, once they move on for whatever reason, we wind up feeling empty and often get involved in the first thing that will give us that same joy! In reality, we need to be like Francine, one of my former students' mom.

When her only son graduated from high school, she joined him after the ceremony they exchanged gifts. She took her roses from him and handed him an envelope with fifteen hundred dollars in it. He looked happily confused as she said, "Your Dad and I are on our way to the airport for a vacation. We have changed the locks and the alarm code, so you won't be able to get back in the house until we get back. Since you have to be at camp on Tuesday, you should be fine." With that said, she kissed him, got one more hug, and left!

Now you may be grabbing your chest wondering how a mother could do that to her child on their Graduation Day, but that's the mindset that you will have to fight to develop, so...

GIRL, GO EAT A COOKIE...AND THEN HANDLE BUSINESS!

As hard as it may be, your Graduation Day won't come until you start preparing for it. One thing I loved about Francine was that she started planning that vacation on the first day of her son's senior year and had it paid for by Spring Break!

Did she agonize about him being away from home? Sure, she did, but she also took the time to build a support network around him where he was going. She found a church, mentoring programs, and things like that to help keep him on track and he didn't see it as her being overbearing. In fact, her doing so kept him out of trouble and he ended up finishing school early because of who she had around him!

This is a crucial time for you because you will soon have more time on your hands that you never knew existed. When you get to the workbook, you're going to see an exercise or two that's going to help you wrangle this time in and use it wisely. It's important that you use this time to get your head together about life after Graduation Day.

We expect our babies to know what they are going to do and badger them to come up with a plan because we don't want them in our houses forever, but we don't have the same plan for ourselves when they do and then put their plan into action.

I remember my mother-in-law intentionally moving into a smaller place after her last child left home. She did so to let them know that it was time for them to be as grown as they told her they were. Downsizing is a common after Graduation Day action!

Other decisions you usually make at this time is finishing your education, starting a business, changing jobs or even going back into the workforce, or taking that needed vacation. It's all about you moving on to the next stage of your life, too! I'm in NO way saying that it's easy, but it is necessary.

"But, Tammie, everyone won't have that kind of Graduation Day." You're right as I am one of them. I have one child in my home whom I know we will always have to care for, so things look a little different for us, too; however, I am still making strides in the things that I want to do as a wife, mother, Christian, and business woman where I can! Ask yourself how you can do the same.

Graduation Day is a reward for all of the labor that you've put in throughout your life, faith, family, ministry, education, business, or career.

When it comes to your faith, you hope and pray to God that you are able to have this same testimony, as difficult as that might be, because faith and ministry can throw you some lean times that make you want to forget you were EVER saved a day in your LIFE! Yet, you know that God and His Holy Spirit are there to help you navigate the labyrinth of dealing with both His creations and His children, as there IS a difference!

You do what you do for the glory of God, knowing that you will never be lauded, appreciated, nor rewarded here on Earth, so this eternal hope is all that you have. You have a scriptural reason to be spiritually extra for Jesus and you want those crowns, or high marks, on your Graduation Day.

"What does that even mean?" It means that you care enough about people that, no matter how they treat you, you show them God's love, which is DIFFERENT from grace! You will have times when you have to let people go and let God deal with them after you've done everything that He has told and led you to do. When there is nothing left, you better take your obedience certificate and move on before you get caught in the crossfire! There is somewhere else to go and something else to do for someone else who God needs you to serve, so GO!

The same applies to business and career. Graduation Day may mean that your time in that business or career is either done completely or it's time to go to the next level.

You could be at the point where you need more people, a bigger building, better technology, or more automation to keep up with things getting better. Or, it could be that it's time to close or hand the business off to the next generation and enjoy rest from your labor.

If you are working, it could be time to retire from that company and move on or take a higher position. It could be that you've been taking required action steps toward something better and Graduation Day means that you have finally done everything you need to do and it's time to go!

Finally, Graduation Day in your education means that you FINALLY did it despite all of the obstacles that you've faced throughout your journey. Whether in person or virtual, you have finished the course and the crown is that degree that will proudly hang on your wall...after you flash it in a few people's faces who thought you'd never make it.

The ultimate Graduation Day is joining our Father in Heaven and the loved ones He called before us. That is a day that many fear and long for at the same time...All we can do is keep doing what He has asked of us to the best of our ability and keep at it until He starts to let us know that our time is at hand.

I do hope and pray that this journey of reading has lit an unquenchable fire under you to handle business in all areas of your life.

I won't say that I've mastered them all myself, but I know that I'm allowed to be a masterpiece and work in progress at the same time.

It is by the grace of God that we are allowed to live, move, and have our being.

Graduation Day...Finally! Now, I want you to go to grab your cookie, go to the workbook for the last time, and empty out until you feel the need to take a deep breath—then keep going!

Now What Business Do You Need to Handle?

You've reached the end of the book and I'm proud of you, but I know that you have a lot weighing on your mind at this point and I want you to take a minute and sit with that.

What is it that you need to do in your life, faith, family, ministry, education, business, or career right now to get the cinder blocks off your shoulders and your feet out of the cement they're encased within?

"Tammie, I honestly don't know... Can we talk about it?" We sure can! You can visit my website at http://everywomanisabusinesswoman.me and leave me a message on the contact page.

Why THAT page? That's the one where I give you the tips, tools, products, and services that you need so that you can start to get ready for your Graduation Day in a few of these areas!

You're worth the time, money, and effort of doing so...and so are your dreams, goals, and aspirations!

About the Author

Tammie T. Polk is a daughter of the King and a married homeschooling mother of three girls, who are 17, 13, and 8. Two of her daughters have special needs, but she and her husband, Elrico, are blessed to be able to care for them in their home!

Professionally, Tammie works as a speaker, Goal and Dream Fulfillment Coach, and author of over 130 print, digital, and audio books and planners—all written and published since September 2015. Her personal mantra is "I write my way through life and business and writing is my cross."

Known as both a sweetheart and a goofball, Tammie believes in showing women what is possible and "lovingly annoys" them to greatness by helping them to eliminate excuses and excel in life and business and take a break from reality in life and business when needed.

When she's not terrorizing her clients or keeping the lights on at Amazon, you'll find her playing mobile, console, PC, or board games, watching police crime dramas or WWE Wrestling, and eating cookies—she's an oatmeal raisin girl at heart!

To learn more about Tammie as:

- A speaker-- http://www.tammieterrellmompreneurs.com
- Goal and Dream Fulfillment Coach – http://www.professionallysassy.me

- Author
  - http://amazon.com/author/tammiepolk
  - http://www.professionallysassy.me/new-products (for in-stock, autographed copies of books)
  - http://www.payhip.com/professionallysassybusinesswoman (audio books)

Other Books by Tammie T. Polk

Listed in order of publication and some grouped by collection

1. #prayandponder: Charges. Choices. Consequences -- From Hebrews to Armageddon

2. #prayandponder: Charges. Choices. Consequences -- Paul and Peter

3. #prayandponder: Charges. Choices. Consequences -- From Jesus to Paul

4. #prayandponder: Charges. Choices. Consequences -- The Gospels

5. #prayandponder: Charges. Choices. Consequences -- Nehemiah and Malachi

6. #prayandponder: Charges. Choices. Consequences -- The Prophets and Esther

7. #prayandponder: Charges. Choices. Consequences -- Joel and Daniel

8. #prayandponder: Charges. Choices. Consequences -- The Lamentations of Ezekiel and the Visions of Ezekiel

9. #prayandponder: Charges. Choices. Consequences -- Psalms, Kings, and Prophets: Volume 1

10. Audio Books

- A Winning Business Season
- Grace, Naps and Cookies (3 parts)
- Chics Who Execute
- Lean Times Aren't Always Financial
- I Write My Way Through Life...You Can, Too!
- Lovingly Annoying You to Greatness: I AM the Worst Case Scenario
- Whose Moment Are You Having?
- Married Woman/Single Woman: Same Issues
- Rebuilding Mai
- Natalynn's Heart: The Comeback
- Share My World: Her Life for Mine
- Creating Your Own Pandemic: "It's Going to Get Better"
- How to Overcome THE Blues: Dealing with Difficult People
- Attack of the Enemy vs. Not in God's Will
- Individuality Chameleon
- All That Knowledge and A Housewife
- From the Heart of a Motherless Daughter
- The Virtuous SINGLE Business Woman
- A Business Woman Has GOALS
- Serious Seconds
- The Title

- God Said, "Write, Daughter!": How My Obedience to Writing Blessed My Business
- The Virtuous Teacher: Proverbs 31 in the Classroom
- Sweetheart and a Goofball: Tammie Loves the Kids
- My Love Affair with Police Crime Dramas
- Game On: Growing Up with Games
- When Your Writing Makes Them Mad
- My Mom: The First Entrepreneur I Ever Saw

11. The Dynamically Different Year
12. What Winners Understand
13. Back to Me: Getting YOU Back
14. Becoming Sassily Me: Confidence and Power Journal
15. Becoming Sassily Me: Acknowledging and Regaining Lost Power
16. The Five Figure Woman
17. Mama, Can We Talk About...
18. Passing Your Torch
19. Are You Getting Enough Fruit
20. Have You Created a Monster
21. From the Staff List to Entrepreneur
22. #prayandponder: C3 -- 2 Samuel, Psalms, and the Chronicles of David
23. From a Phoenix to an Ant
24. Wallflower
25. Every Woman Is A Business Woman Workbook
26. Professionally Sassy Business Woman

76. You Are A Franchise: You Did Know that Right?

77. The Revelated Church

78. Every Woman Is a Business Woman Boot Camp Planner

79. Woman on a Mission

80. #prayandponder: Volume 1

81. Warrior Women

82. Becoming Mai

83. Rise Reclaim Evolve NOW

84. Personal Perspective Project/#ShadeDisguised

85. Being PIRRPEARED

86. The Last Escapade

87. Every Woman Is a Business Woman Boot Camp

88. Slaying the Slayers to Become A Virtuous Business Woman

89. The Real Business Women Slay Slayers Super Books

- Broken Business Woman
- Time Constrained Business Woman
- Job Insecure Business Woman
- Sad and Settled Business Woman
- One Hit Wonder Business Woman
- Family Distracted Business Woman
- Talent Starved Business Woman

90. Prayerfully Paying Attention

91. Getting Rid of That Babypreneur Mentality

92. Putting Your Choices in Check

93. The Distinguished Business Man

94. The Virtuous Business Woman Workbook

Made in the USA
Columbia, SC
08 July 2022

63067774R00036